A VICTORIAN CHRISTMAS

Brian Williams

PITKIN

Victorian Christmas Cheer

At the darkest time of the northern year comes the most joyous of festivals – Christmas. For Christians celebrating the birth of Christ, and for those of other faiths and none, Christmas is a season of magical expectation and delights.

Yet before the 19th century, Christmas in Britain was a shadow of the brash, extravagant festival we know today. The Twelve Days of Christmas, from St Stephen's Day (26 December) to Epiphany (6 January), passed without much public show. Gifts were not given until New Year, and for most people Christmas Day was one day's holiday at best. For many it was a working day like any other.

The Victorians reinvented the festive season. An ancient winter festival absorbed by the Church evolved yet again – to blend sentiment, commerce and fun into the Victorian Christmas aglow with candle-lit trees, cards and crackers, Santa Claus and toys, carols and Christmas pudding. The Victorians helped make the modern Christmas a celebration of family and love, its sparkling trappings transforming mid-winter gloom into the most heart-warming time of the year.

A Winter Festival

The fact that Christmas falls at the time of the northern winter solstice is no coincidence.

The exact date of Christ's birth is not known. The calendar date of 25 December was set by the Church in Rome in the mid-4th century, possibly aligned with the Roman midwinter festival of Saturnalia. Earlier, Christians may have marked the nativity of Christ on 6 January, now known as Epiphany, the twelfth and last day of Christmas.

Cheering Dark Days

Saturnalia was celebrated by the Romans in December, with feasting and boisterousness. People partied, dressed up, decorated their homes with greenery and exchanged presents. Later northern European festivals marked the changing seasons. Yule celebrated the winter solstice, when most trees were bare, skies grey, the days short, and the sun rarely warmed the chilled earth. Plants were dead or dormant. At this time, people lit bonfires and drank ale, to cheer themselves. Pagan priests cut mistletoe from sacred oaks. Yule logs burned on hearths to drive away the spirits of darkness and ensure the return of the sun.

The Church Calendar

The Christian Church deftly inserted Christmas into this traditional feast. In England, Christmas Day (25 December on the Gregorian calendar) became the focus for religious celebration. Elsewhere in Europe, Christmas Eve was more central to religious observance, and in the Orthodox churches, which stuck to

The Victorian Christmas became a warm, gift-giving family celebration, its customs followed by later generations.

the Julian calendar, the date of Christmas remains 7 January. Advent, heralding the start of the Christmas season, begins in the western liturgical calendar on the fourth Sunday before Christmas Day, but Advent calendars and candles start from 1 December.

Below: Advent calendars were first printed in Germany in the late 1800s.

The Holly King

Holly was central to old midwinter customs. The Holly King was a figure from pre-Christian midwinter mythology, full of life and cheer, but he had a darker side, in constant yearly battle with his summer rival, the Oak. The Holly King had a Queen, represented by ivy.

DECEMBER.
Sun. 1 8 -15 22 29
Mon. 2 9 16 23 30
Tue. 3 10 17 24 31
Wed. 4 11 18 25 ✳
Thu. 5 12 19 26 ✳
Fri. 6 13 20 27 ✳
Sat. 7 14 21 28 ✳

Thou crownest the year with Thy goodness.
Psa. 65. 11.

Love will meet with thought divine Every need of yours and mine.
Charlotte Murray.

Deck the Halls...

Gathering evergreens to 'deck the halls' has a long association with Christmas.

Other plants were, and still are, brought into the home at Christmas to add colour and aroma. However, the plants most people associated with Christmas (apart from the Christmas tree) were holly, ivy and mistletoe.

The Holly and the Ivy

At the point of the year when most trees in the northlands were bare, the evergreens, and particularly holly with its bright red berries, were symbols of hope, rebirth and the return of fertility. The Christian Church borrowed the custom from the old pagan traditions, bringing evergreens indoors at Christmas to symbolise the birth, life and resurrection of Christ. Some believers held that the crown of thorns worn by Christ at the crucifixion was made of holly, the berries reddened by Christ's blood. Thus, in the words of 'The Holly and the Ivy', an old carol among those 'rescued' and revived by the Victorians, 'the holly bears the crown'. Holly and ivy were woven into wreaths and swags, and Victorian vicars even published guidance on how best to decorate the church, both for a pleasing appearance, and to hide some of the less attractive features of their buildings.

Ivy was usually easier to find. It was also more adaptable and could be wound around picture frames, candlesticks, or banisters. Other plants such as rosemary, bay and lavender also found their way into the Christmas home. Harder to collect, since it often grows high on the host trees to which it clings as a semi-parasite, is mistletoe.

In theory, a mistletoe berry was plucked for each kiss. No more berries, and the kissing stopped!

Beneath the Mistletoe

Mistletoe was a plant of mysterious ambiguity. Long associated with pre-Christian Druidism, mistletoe was linked to fertility. Another name for it was 'all-heal', and sprigs of the plant hung above doors to protect a family from harm. Yet, in Norse myth, the mistletoe was associated with death.

Kiss Me Quick!

Overseas visitors were at times surprised by the English lack of reserve when it came to 'mistletoe-kissing'. The American writer Nathaniel Hawthorne was amused, or shocked, while staying at a boarding house in Southport by the boldness of the maidservants – who drew gentlemen into the kitchen, where bunches of mistletoe hung from the gas lights.

A dart of mistletoe killed Balder, best-loved son of the supreme god Odin. It was thrown by the blind god Hod, tricked by the wicked Loki, as mistletoe alone could kill Balder. Later, mistletoe became a love-symbol equated with Cupid's dart, finding a new use in the 'kissing ring', or 'kissing bough' of mistletoe, beneath which anyone could be kissed. Hence the custom of hanging it up over a doorway, to welcome guests.

The Yule Log

Burning a log on Christmas Eve was a reminder of ancient midwinter traditions. 'Yule' was a Germanic name for the festival, and the yule log was a symbol of warmth and hope. The log was burned to bring good luck to the household. A small piece of the log was kept, as kindling for the new year. Today, 'bringing in the yule' is more often represented by a cake, the chocolate log made to resemble the yule log of old.

The Royal Christmas

In 1819, when only seven months old, Princess Victoria arrived to spend Christmas in Devon with her parents, the Duke and Duchess of Kent.

The Kents had chosen Sidmouth over London for their Christmas, during a winter of unusual severity, and arrived on Christmas Day, after what must have been a taxing journey, in a snowstorm. The Duke, 53 and previously robust, caught a cold, developed pneumonia, and died on 23 January. Six days later, the Duke's father George III died, and Victoria's uncle, the Prince Regent, became King George IV.

The young princess was by modern ideas a lonely child; her affectionate half-sister Feodora (12 years her senior) escaped what she called 'imprisonment' in Kensington Palace in 1828, by marrying a German prince. Most of Victoria's Christmases were spent with her mother, and her governess, Louise Lehzen. The death of her uncle William IV in 1837 left Victoria as Queen, at 18.

Married Christmases

Christmases for Queen Victoria were happier after her marriage in 1840. Her husband (and cousin) Albert of Saxe-Coburg-Gotha enjoyed

On the ice at Frogmore (Windsor) Albert skated, pushing the Queen in an 'ice-chair'.

Jumping for Joy

In 1850 Queen Victoria wrote in her journal of her children's pleasure in their Christmas presents. 'The 7 children were then taken to their tree, jumping and shouting with joy over their toys and other presents: the boys could think of nothing but the swords we had given them and Bertie some of the armour, which however he complained, pinched him.'

Christmas, and the addition of babies also transformed family celebrations. The Queen's first married Christmas was at Windsor, with her first baby (Victoria, Princess Royal) just over a month old. For the second (1841), the Queen had produced a male heir (Edward, Prince of Wales). Christmas became a time for children, games, dressing-up and gift-giving. The gifts were set out on tables, beneath Christmas trees, at Windsor Castle. In the German tradition, the royal couple exchanged presents on Christmas Eve, and the Prince taught the children to wish their mother a good New Year, in German.

Family Feasts

Albert made economies in the Royal Household, but there was plenty to enjoy. In 1860, a visitor to Windsor at Christmas recorded 50 turkeys roasting in the kitchen, and a woodcock pie containing 100 birds. Charlotte Canning (a lady-in-waiting) reported a 'great deal of feasting', enormous meats and pies, and 'German trees with sugar plums and presents given to everybody'. In the snow, Albert drove the Queen and their children in a sleigh. Osborne House on the Isle of Wight (first occupied in 1846) offered winter delights too: a slide 'used by young and old' wrote the Queen, 'and a splendid snow-man'.

Above: In 1848 the royal Christmas tree appeared in the Illustrated London News. *The royal example was followed across the land.*

The Christmas Tree

Christmas trees were first known as 'German trees'.

In Germany, the Christmas tree was a Protestant Christmas tradition; Catholics in much of Europe usually setting up a Nativity crib. Prince Albert is often credited with introducing 'German trees' to Windsor Castle, but a yew tree had been set up at Christmas in 1800 by Queen Charlotte, wife of George III, and decorated trees were found in great houses, often for children's parties, and lit with candles. In Germany, fir and spruce trees were often trimmed into boughs and fronds but in Britain people liked a whole tree.

Royal Trees

For Albert, the Christmas tree was a reminder of home and childhood. Victoria had also seen Christmas trees as a child; her journal for Christmas Eve 1832 (when she was 13) recalls that her mother, the Duchess of Kent, had ordered two trees for Kensington Palace. Victoria was entranced by the lights and sugar ornaments. She had one tree to herself – the other was for the family of Sir John Conroy, who ran her mother's household.

The royal couple's first tree at Windsor Castle in 1840 was the forerunner of many. Prince Albert wrote to his father to describe the joy of the Princess Royal and the Prince of Wales, his two oldest children, 'full of happy wonder' as they gazed at the candle-lit tree. The Windsor Castle trees were not always floor-standing; in 1860 a visitor to the Castle described how the rooms 'were lighted up with Christmas trees hung from the ceiling, the chandeliers being taken down. These trees...were covered with bonbons and little wax coloured lights, some of the trees were made to appear as if partially covered in snow.'

Spruced Up Trees

Trees were first decorated with candles, sugar mice, ribbons and paper

Candles

Christmas tree candles were fixed to branches with melted wax or pins, before candle-holders were sold. Victorians were used to candles – and doubtless kept watch lest the tree burst into flames! By the late 19th century, trendsetters could lease trees with electric 'fairy lights'.

New York claimed the first electrically lit Christmas tree in 1882.

twists. Tinsel (strips of metal, originally silver) soon became popular, and advertisements for tree decorations began appearing in the 1850s. Most trees were imported until the 1880s, when home-grown Norway spruces became available. Shortage of small real trees led to German firms selling artificial trees in the 1880s; either a wooden pyramid, or a frame stuck with painted goose feathers.

Dickens and Christmas

When Princess Victoria was born in 1819, some people already lamented the decline of the English Christmas.

The age of reason, with its revolutionary ideas, had challenged religion and old customs linked to 'superstition'. Social and industrial changes were equally radical. That Christmas bounced back, and took on the form we recognize, owed not a little to the century's most famous writer: Charles Dickens.

Christmas Tales

Dickens loved Christmas, for its warmth and good cheer. In *The Pickwick Papers* (1837), his first big success, Mr Pickwick himself, and 'Christmas at Dingley Dell', glowed with conviviality. The writer struck a serious note with *A Christmas Carol* in 1843, perhaps influenced by *Punch* magazine's 'How Mr Chokepear Keeps a Merry Christmas'. A complacent churchgoing consumer of mince pies and custards, Mr Chokepear was indeed merry but had cut off his daughter for marrying beneath her and ignored the shivering poor on his doorstep. Was this, the magazine questioned, 'the Christmas of a good man'?

Enter Ebenezer Scrooge

Primed by such questions, the world was ready for Scrooge. *A Christmas Carol* has become perhaps the classic Christmas tale. It took Christmas from the countryside to London, a city of wealthy financiers, struggling clerks, and miserable poor. Dickens' novella

Above: Mr Fezziwig, Scrooge's former
employer, embodies all that is cheerful and
generous in the Christmas spirit.
Left: Bob Cratchit with Tiny Tim.

The Cratchits' Christmas

'There never was such a goose. Bob
said he didn't believe there ever was
such a goose cooked. Its tenderness
and flavour, size and cheapness, were
the themes of universal admiration.
Eked out by apple-sauce and mashed
potatoes, it was a sufficient dinner
for the whole family... In half a
minute Mrs. Cratchit entered —
flushed, but smiling proudly — with
the pudding, like a speckled cannon-
ball, so hard and firm, blazing in half
of half-a-quartern of ignited brandy,
and bedight with Christmas holly
stuck into the top.'

Charles Dickens, *A Christmas Carol*

sold 15,000 copies in its first year;
there were simultaneously nine London
theatre versions, and people read it
aloud, like the Bible. In Scrooge, Bob
Cratchit and his son Tiny Tim, and in
the presentation of three Christmases
(Past, Present, and Yet to Come),
Dickens tapped into a new moral
mood. His book set abundance
against want, cold-heartedness
against neighbourliness.
Scrooge is saved – by
Christmas.

The success of *A Christmas
Carol*, and the writer's
lifelong enthusiasm for
Christmas, helped to create the
'Dickensian Christmas' recycled by

*'Would that Christmas
lasted the whole year
through...'*

Charles Dickens, in
Sketches by Boz (1836)

film-makers, advertisers and
illustrators – a cosy world of
blazing fires, candle-lit parlours,
well-filled plates, hot punch
and smiling faces. As the
novelist knew only too well,
this was no more 'real' than
are Victorian Christmas card
images of gas-lit streets, carol-
singers in crinolines, and horse-
drawn coaches outside country inns.

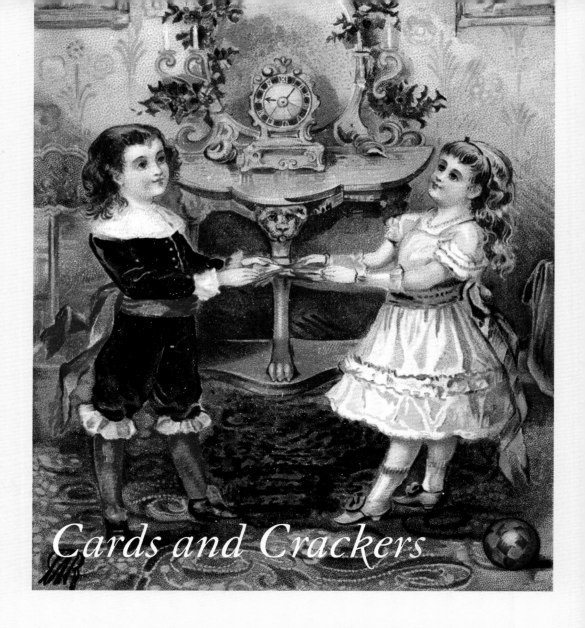

Cards and Crackers

Christmas was changed for ever by the Christmas card.

There is debate as to the first, but credit usually goes to Sir Henry Cole (director of what became the Victoria and Albert Museum in South Kensington). In 1843, Cole asked the artist J. C. Horsley to design a Christmas greetings card, and a thousand illustrated cards were printed. Some were for Cole's use; the rest sold at a shilling a time (not cheap).

Post Plenty for Christmas

The idea caught on. More cards went on sale, and people took advantage of the recent 'penny post' (1840) to send a card anywhere in the country. Favourite early cards showed family and rural life, but religious images also featured (the Nativity, the wise men, angels and shepherds) along with secular pictures (horses, cats, flowers, comic scenes). Images of children became hugely popular, as did now-familiar Christmas card icons, such as plum pudding, holly, bells, Christmas trees,

Just a scrap of paper
Yet its message hear
Ever and for ever
Shall I love thee, dear

Motto from a Tom Smith cracker

Father Christmas, and snow. The robin, symbolic of the postman, was often shown carrying cards or perched on a letterbox.

By 1880 more than 11 million Christmas cards were posted, most carried by Britain's railways.

In 1870 a halfpenny post cut the cost of sending greetings. Improvements in colour printing made cards attractive yet affordable 'remembrances' to post to family and friends. The Victorians loved the sentimental, and Christmas cards indulged that love to the full. The Queen encouraged her children to make their own cards, and children across the land did the same.

Christmas Crackers

Inspired by a visit to France, where he had enjoyed 'bon-bons' (sugared almonds wrapped in paper), crackers were the brainchild of a London sweetshop owner called Tom Smith. In 1847, he started selling them, adding a 'love-motto' inside. He replaced the almonds with small gifts in 1850,

Above: The first Christmas card (1843) showed three generations of a family toasting an absent friend, surrounded by images of charitable giving.

eyeing the growing Christmas market. Another brainwave came in the 1860s. Inspired by logs crackling on a fire, he added a 'snap' inside a cardboard tube.

Boxed sets of crackers were soon hugely popular. In 1880, Tom Smith died, and one of his sons, Walter, is credited with adding paper hats to the cracker's contents. Upmarket crackers contained real jewels, but most were cheap and cheerful, and cracker and contents (snap, joke, gift, motto, hat) have remained little changed into the 21st century.

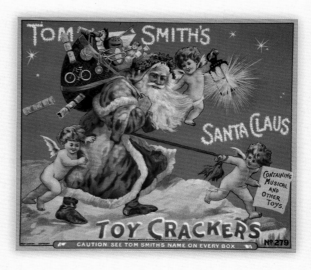

Right: In this Christmas cracker advertisement, Santa enlists the aid of cherubs, rather than elves!

Victorian Carols

Some of our best-loved carols were first sung during the Victorian era. Old carols were revived, and new ones composed.

Many old carols were regional; neither exclusively religious, nor sung only at Christmas. Some had been sung to accompany religious dramas as early as the 1300s. In England, choral singing flourished until after the English Civil War, when carols were threatened by Puritan distaste for the 'frivolities' of Christmas. The reign of Charles I restored merriment, but in the 1700s Christmas lost some of its vigour, and by Victoria's reign there were fears that

carols were in danger of dying out. That they did not was largely due to song-collectors.

Carol Collectors

William Sandys, Davies Gilbert MP, E. F. Rimbault and others toured the countryside listening to old people's songs. In 1841 Thomas Wright in *Specimens of Old Christmas Carols* traced the carol back to the Anglo-Saxons. This, and the medieval flavour of many carols, attuned with the Victorians' love of 'Olde England'.

The collectors' zeal, and Victorian hymn-writers, brought about a carol revival. Old ones were revived, including such modern favourites as Wesley's 'Hark! the Herald Angels Sing'. From the 1840s, numerous carol collections included Neale and Helmond's *Carols for Christmas-tide* (1853), and Bramley and Stainer's *Christmas Carols New and Old* (1869). The Church of England included carols in its 1861 *Hymns Ancient and Modern*.

New Words, Old Tunes

New carols were often set to familiar tunes, and sung not just in churches, but at home, in schools and on the streets by carol-singers. Many carols reinforced the idea that Christmas celebrated not just Christ's birth, but childhood itself – in the words of 'Once in Royal David's City' (by Mrs C. F. Alexander, 1848): 'Christian children all must be Mild, obedient, good as He...'

Carol services in church, and carol concerts in other public places, only really became popular in late Victorian times. The first 'Festival of Nine Lessons and Carols' was reputedly held in 1880 at Truro when the cathedral choir moved their Christmas Eve service indoors, having previously sung in the city streets.

The Waits

Waits were bands of musicians and singers who performed in the street. Medieval waits had been in some places the 'town band'. Victorian performers attracted less praise than complaint: that they sang the same two or three carols, to one tune, and disturbed the peace late at night.

New Favourites

Carols first sung in Victorian times, though not all composed in Britain, include: 'O Come All Ye Faithful' (1843) and 'Once in Royal David's City' (1848). 'O Little Town of Bethlehem' (1868) was written in North America, as was 'Away in a Manger' (1883). 'While Shepherds Watched Their Flocks by Night' was originally a hymn and was sung to several tunes.

Christmas Fare

The traditional Christmas fare in England was meat: beef, venison, goose, game birds large and small, and (the classic centrepiece) a boar's head, carried in with great ceremony.

Goose was the most visible festive treat, with pre-Christmas flocks of geese being driven to market. Market towns held cattle shows just before Christmas, the prize beefs displayed in butchers' shops.

Goose vs Turkey

Poulterers displayed racks of geese and turkeys. Poorer families paid into 'goose clubs' to save for their Christmas dinner – one such club features in the Sherlock Holmes story *The Blue Carbuncle*. Christmas clubs proved popular, with pub landlords offering alcohol, rather than a goose, and continued to thrive into the next century. Turkey became the main rival to the Christmas goose. Still, many poorer families made do with chicken (otherwise a rare treat), beef or pork.

The Christmas Feast

In the week before Christmas, markets hummed with activity. Wagons rattled in from ports and farms, to stock the shops. Barrowloads of apples, pears, grapes, pineapples, pomegranates, medlars, cobnuts and filberts were trundled through streets. Shoppers

Workhouse Christmas

Workhouse food was kept meagre, but there were charitable seasonal gestures. Workhouse inmates in Liverpool, for instance, were served Christmas dinner of beef and plum pudding. Workhouse guardians and locals paid for small gifts: tobacco and ale for adults; fruit, nuts, sweets and cheap toys for children. In some towns the 'workhouse Christmas' became something of a civic event.

In 1860 the chef at Windsor Castle cooked 50 turkeys, and a bowl of mincemeat laced with two dozen bottles of brandy.

were tempted by sweets, chocolates, and biscuits, colourfully packaged to catch the eye.

Puddings and Pies

An old favourite was 'Christmas porridge': one recipe suggested beef broth thickened with bread, to which the cook added prunes, raisins, currants, spices and wine. This was a variant of the medieval frumenty, or furmity. Christmas porridge was still being eaten in the 1840s, and traditionally made on 22 December. The plum or 'figgy' pudding was a suet pudding flavoured with currants, raisins, eggs, breadcrumbs, nutmeg and sugar, and then steamed in a cloth. The last Sunday before Advent was 'Stir-up Sunday', when adults and children took turns to stir the Christmas pudding, for luck. A wooden spoon was essential, as was clockwise stirring. A coin was often added to the mixture, and whoever found it on Christmas Day was extra-lucky.

The 'mincemeat' in a Victorian mince pie was meat mixed with beef suet, dried and fresh fruits, citrus peel, almonds, sugar and spices – plus sherry, brandy or port. Today, the meat has disappeared. Mincemeat was supposed to be made on 1 December; and eating 12 mince pies before Christmas Day was said to bring good luck all year! The impressive Yorkshire Christmas pie was stuffed with meat: turkey, goose, chicken, rabbit, pheasant, partridge, ham and tongue.

The Boar's Head

The boar's head was honoured in a 15th-century carol. According to legend, in 1340 a scholar of Queen's College, Oxford, was attacked by a wild boar, but thrust a book (Aristotle) down its throat. The boar's head ended up on the College's Christmas table, and the boar's head feast is still celebrated at Queen's College.

Home for the Holiday

Many workers had a rare day off on 25 December, which encouraged the Chartists in 1838 to pick Christmas Day for a protest march.

People went to church, but in the early part of Victoria's reign, life went on much as on any other day, though the better-off might invite guests to dine, or throw a 'juvenile party'. Business as usual continued, and government ministers would often hold meetings on Christmas Day.

In the country, with farms at their least active outdoors, 'Christmas' extended for the Twelve Days, and many did not take down decorations until Plough Monday, the Monday after Epiphany (6 January). In some areas Christmas lasted until Candlemas (2 February). The factory calendar was different; a Christmas break left machines idle, and so hit production.

Boxing Day

St Stephen's Day, 26 December, became Boxing Day, when boxes were put out for 'tips' or rewards for deserving servants and tradespeople. Domestic staff were allowed the day off after toiling through Christmas Day. Soliciting a 'Christmas box', *Punch* magazine found, was so common that householders were pestered by 'raps at the door and pulls at the bell' from all and sundry.

The extended Christmas shut-down of modern times would have startled the Victorians. Their Christmas was brief, and busy. New bank holiday laws (1871 and 1875) fixed Boxing Day as one of four public holidays in England, Wales and Ireland (with Easter Monday, Whit Monday, and August Bank Holiday Monday).

Left: A Christmas train disgorges passengers and baggage on the Eastern Counties Railway, opened 1839. Others dashed through the snow in traditional coaching style (above).

Scots took New Year's Day instead, celebrating Hogmanay.

Christmas Getaway

Seasonal family reunions became part of the Victorian Christmas, thanks to the rapid spread of the railways. Busy stations became a seasonal symbol, and so too did the happy homecoming. However, it was no longer enough to hang up a few boughs of evergreens and holly. The home must have decorations, and Christmas fare with novel delicacies prepared from recipes. In books and magazines, 'experts' informed readers that a little trouble (and expense) would increase festive enjoyment. It was the start of a trend that developed into a pre-Christmas avalanche of suggestions for out-Christmassing your friends!

Christmas in the Colonies

Readers at home were treated to accounts of Christmas around the British Empire – from the snows of Canada to the hot sun of India, Australia, South Africa, and Egypt. Everywhere, Britishers abroad did their best to recreate Christmas at home, toasting the Queen and eating tinned Christmas puddings shipped from England.

Father Christmas

Father Christmas emerged from misty origins. As the 'Spirit of Christmas' he began to make his presence felt from the 1850s, initially more as a Falstaff-like Lord of Misrule, offering pudding and a bottle, than as the bringer of gifts for children.

His appearance was sombre, in a brown, white or yellow robe, with a crown of holly – reminiscent, some thought, of the Norse god Odin, who wore a hooded cloak on his visits to mankind.

Enter Santa

From the 1850s, the old English Father Christmas morphed into Santa Claus. Santa Claus took his name from a 4th-century bishop of Smyrna (Turkey), St Nicholas, who became a popular saint in medieval Europe, especially in Italy. Nicholas left presents of food or money in the stockings of needy children, and he was adopted in northern Europe as 'Santa Claus' ('Sinterklaas' in Dutch).

He featured in an 1809 story by the American author Washington Irving, and reappeared in Clement Clarke Moore's 1822 'A Visit from St. Nicholas', the poem that begins: 'Twas the night before Christmas...', though this was not published in Britain until 1891. By the 1860s, the now-familiar persona was appearing, as pictured many times by the German-born American illustrator Thomas Nast: a white-bearded grandfather-figure in red suit or cloak, and boots, with sled, sack and reindeer.

Onto the High Street

Some Victorian churchgoers had mixed views about this semi-pagan character inveigling himself into the Christmas story, and into people's homes by way of chimneys. However, his essential benevolence, and generosity towards 'good' children, won the day. Writing a Christmas list to Santa, and leaving a tempting morsel for him on Christmas Eve, became for most children an essential part of Christmas.

By the end of the 19th century, Father Christmas/ Santa Claus had moved from the chimney to the department store, holding court in his grotto to dispense gifts and good cheer. In the 1870s, Lewis's Bon Marché in Liverpool, one of the new department stores, opened a 'Christmas fairyland', and Father Christmas reposed in Fortnum & Mason in London by 1898. Before long in almost every high street, a child could meet Father Christmas in person, and the post office was used to receiving letters addressed to him c/o the North Pole.

Children hung up stockings, in the hope that Father Christmas would visit. Somehow, he – and his sack of toys – would negotiate the chimney, while his sled and reindeer waited on the roof. Many poor children made do with a stocking containing an orange, nuts and sweets.

Right: A classic interpretation of Santa Claus as the white-bearded grandfather-figure, wearing a red cloak and holding a gift-filled sack.

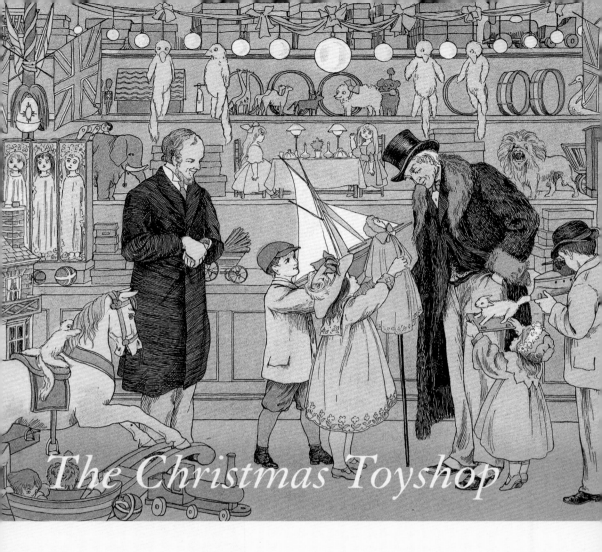

The Christmas Toyshop

Shopping for Christmas gifts took off in the mid-1800s, with developments in advertising, factory production, and new kinds of shops, including the first large department stores.

Before the 1880s, no one started Christmas shopping until December (in the 1850s it had been more usually a week before). Now people were urged to shop earlier, with retailers offering seasonal treats six weeks or more before Christmas, as they promoted Christmas offers of 'novelties' such as portrait albums, scrap books, clocks, purses, jewel cases, games and 'nic-nacs'. Upmarket retailers began offering customers Christmas hampers and 'fancy boxes' of delights – scent bottles, crackers, cards and tree decorations.

Gift-Giving

By the 1890s Christmas advertisements were appearing in the newspapers before the end of November. In Victorian towns and cities, many shops stayed open late, so the last-minute rush was part of the fun. Presents were traditionally exchanged on Boxing Day or New Year, when maidservants received gifts (typically a cap with ribbons) and children had pencil cases, pen knives and books. The new parcel post (1883) encouraged gift-sending. Country folk sent

'Myself or the Children?' This print from 1872 shows a workman gazing longingly at a Christmas window display.

poultry, butter, cream and other delicacies to relations in town. Prince Albert believed gift-giving showed affection, and the royal family exchanged Christmas presents with much delight. The Queen gave presents to her servants on Christmas Eve, usually practical gifts (meat, pies and clothing), with toys, books and clothes for children. Members of the royal household might receive cuff-links, cigarette-cases, jewellery, porcelain – and photographs of the royal family. Family presents came last, and were set out on tables, for Her Majesty to inspect.

Toys for Christmas

As children became the focus of Victorian Christmas sensibilities, toyshops, and toy departments in large stores, enticed customers with tantalising window displays. Most children were still happy with hand-made playthings, but factory-made toys offered a wider range for those families who could afford them: rocking horses, trains, clockwork animals, toy soldiers, Noah's Arks, and sophisticated dolls. Some gifts were 'improving' and educational: alphabet bricks, spelling games, and books with a moral message.

Parlour Games and Mummers

The Victorians made most of their
own entertainment; they sang, played
music, danced, and staged amateur
theatre shows. Christmas was the
perfect time for such pleasures, in the
parlour – usually the warmest room,
apart from the kitchen.

The Queen gave Christmas entertainments for
children at Windsor Castle, where pride of
place often went to the 'Royal Twelfth Cake'.
In 1854 she invited the prime minister, Lord
Aberdeen, to watch the 'happy little people,
including some of his own grandchildren,
enjoying themselves'. Juvenile parties were
part of the middle-class Christmas, usually
with music, dancing and charades, a conjuror
or a magic lantern show.

Family Favourites

In the Victorian parlour, sing-songs and card
games were popular, and so were charades.
New children's games included happy families,
tiddlywinks, ludo and snakes and ladders (the
last two both adapted from Indian originals).
Snap-dragon was a risky game often played
on Christmas Eve. Players had to grab a raisin
from a dish of fruit that had been soaked in
brandy and set alight. In a variant known as
flap-dragon, players had to drink a glass of
ale while holding a lighted candle in their
mouths – perilous for ladies in flammable
dresses and gentlemen with whiskers!

> *'Christmas is coming, the goose is getting fat, Please put a penny in the old man's hat.'*

Civic pride was demonstrated with parties for children, like the Twelfth Night fancy dress balls at the Mansion House in London. These became elaborate affairs with a thousand guests, military bands and variety acts. Other cities followed suit.

Mummers' Plays

Schoolchildren in what was still a predominantly Christian country enacted the Christmas story, beginning the tradition of the school nativity play. But there were other plays too. Masked and costumed 'mummers', or 'guisers', trooped from house to house. The mummers were wild, inventive and hilarious. They often began with a sword dance, followed by action a-plenty: St George fought a Turk, sometimes his Dragon roared in, and the Doctor revived the dead. Various demons demanded money from the audience, the cue for the rhyme 'Christmas is coming...' Good triumphed over evil, and 'Old Sir Christmas' might appear to ask: 'Welcome or welcome not, I hope old Father Christmas will never be forgot.'

Above: Enjoying Little Red Riding Hood. Below: Mummers' plays were inventive and hilarious, with lots of regional variations.

Pantomime

Victorian theatregoers liked sentiment and chilling thrills — and pantomime provided them all.

Pantomimes offered stars, a pacy plot, love songs, melodramatic villains, stage fights, comic turns, performing animals, exotic costumes, and lavish special effects. No wonder audiences flocked to the theatres every year, when pantomimes usually opened on Boxing Day.

The shows developed from the earlier mimed 'harlequinades' featuring Harlequin, Columbine, Pierrot, Pantaloon and Clown, and drew on fairy tales, nursery rhymes and legend for their stories, amazing audiences with 'transformation' scenes.

Thrills and Chills
The Victorians mined nursery tales and legends for Christmas pantomimes. Others survive to this day. Seasonal favourites

Prince of Wales preferred to head for Sandringham. However, in her old age, Christmas was once again a happy, if wistful, family occasion, presided over by the royal grandmother ('Gan-Gan' to the little ones). There were programmes of music and 'tableaux vivants' acted by Court ladies and gentlemen, and children. The initial letter of each scene in the tableaux spelt out the word 'Christmas', and at the finale the royal children brought in the Yule log.

'He's behind you! Oh no, he isn't....'

included *Cinderella, Humpty Dumpty, Jack and the Beanstalk*, and *Aladdin*. This last production introduced Widow Twankey (named after a Chinese tea-port, and a brand of cheap tea), but shows also featured heroic figures, such as Alfred the Great, Richard I, Robin Hood, Nell Gwynne and Good Queen Bess. The 1882 *Sindbad the Sailor* included a pageant of kings and queens, Shakespeare, Guy Fawkes, Napoleon and Wellington, and a rousing parade of imperial soldiers back from Egypt. Stars of the music halls added new lustre to the pantomime, with one of the great 'dames' of the age, the comedian Dan Leno, at London's Drury Lane.

Royal Entertainment

The Queen had her own theatre at Windsor Castle, and loved her Christmas entertainments, which one year (1843) featured a group of Native Americans in war paint. They ceased after the death of Prince Albert in 1860 cast a shadow over all festivities, and in her later years, the Queen spent Christmas at Osborne, though the

Below: A poster for Dick Whittington and His Cat, which played at the Theatre Royal, Drury Lane in 1894.

29

Ring Out the Old

Seeing out the old year, and ringing in the new, was a good excuse for extending the festivities.

Victoria and Albert loved their Scottish home, Balmoral Castle, though were seldom there in midwinter. But both enjoyed Scottish traditions, such as Hogmanay 'first footing', a custom also common in the north of England to bring good luck for the year. The English also had 'letting in Christmas' – when the first person to visit a house on Christmas Day was let in through the front door, and out through the back, receiving gifts as they did so in return for good luck. The Hogmanay first footer was the first person to cross the threshold after midnight at New Year; ideally male and dark-haired, he should bear a piece of coal, plus a coin, shortbread, black bun (a fruit cake covered in pastry) and something to warm the innards, such as a glass of whisky.

Twelfth Night

The Victorian Christmas closed with Twelfth Night, when the decorations were taken down. In the 19th century, and later, to do this earlier was considered unlucky. Nowadays, the decorations frequently go up, and come down, long before dates our Victorian forebears would have considered appropriate.

Traditionally, the last Christmas party was held on Twelfth Night. A Twelfth Night cake was the centrepiece of the event, and inside was a bean. Whoever found the bean led the fun and games, as a latter-day Lord of Misrule. The Twelfth Night cake had been baked since Tudor times; in some recipes, a pea was also hidden inside, for a female guest to find and become the Twelfth Night queen.

Wassailing

A silver wassail bowl at Jesus College, Oxford, reputedly holds 10 gallons!

Wassailing comes from the Anglo-Saxon *waes haile*, meaning 'good health'. On New Year's Day the wassailers gathered in an orchard, usually around midday, and sprinkled the largest apple tree with cider to cries of 'huzzah'. This they did to ensure a good crop. Wassailing was also taken door to door, offering good wishes, and a wassail bowl. At its simplest this contained nuts and spiced ale; at its richest, a frothy mixture of mulled ale, curdled cream, roasted apples, eggs, cloves, ginger, nutmeg and sugar.

Opposite: 'Christmas at Dingley Dell' from Dickens' The Pickwick Papers.

Left: Wassailers on Twelfth Night, raising tankards of mulled cider to apple trees in Devon.

Places to Visit

There is space here to mention only a few of many places that shed light on the Victorians, and what they did for Christmas. They include museums, palaces and historic houses, many of which put on themed events and exhibitions at Christmas.

Beamish, The Living Museum of the North,
County Durham
www.beamish.org.uk

Blists Hill Victorian town,
Telford, Shropshire
www.ironbridge.org.uk/explore/blists-hill-victorian-town/

Buckingham Palace, London SW1 1AA
www.royalcollection.org.uk

Castle Howard, North Yorkshire
www.castlehoward.co.uk

Charles Dickens Museum,
London WC1N 2LX
dickensmuseum.com

Edinburgh Castle
www.edinburghcastle.scot

English Heritage
www.english-heritage.org.uk/christmas/

Historic Scotland
members.historic-scotland.gov.uk/

Museum of Childhood, Edinburgh EH1 1TG
www.edinburghmuseums.org.uk/venue/museum-childhood

National Trust
www.nationaltrust.org.uk/lists/experience-christmas-near-you

National Museums Scotland
www.nms.ac.uk/

Osborne House, Isle of Wight
www.english-heritage.org.uk

Palace of Holyroodhouse,
Edinburgh EH8 8DX
www.royalcollection.org.uk

Ragged School Museum, London E3 4RR
www.raggedschoolmuseum.org.uk

St James's Palace, London SW1A 1BS
www.royal.uk/royal-residences-st-jamess-palace

Standen House, West Sussex
www.nationaltrust.org.uk/standen-house-and-garden

The Workhouse, Southwell, Nottinghamshire
www.nationaltrust.org.uk/the-workhouse-southwell

Tower of London, London EC3N 4AB
www.hrp.org.uk/toweroflondon

Victoria and Albert Museum,
London SW7 2RL
www.vam.ac.uk

V&A Museum of Childhood, London E2 9PA
www.vam.ac.uk/moc/

Warwick Castle
www.warwick-castle.co.uk

Windsor Castle
www.royalcollection.org.uk

York Castle Museum
www.yorkcastlemuseum.org.uk